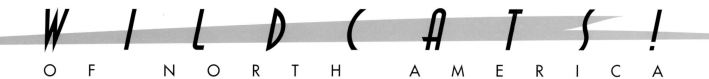

WILDCATS!
OF NORTH AMERICA

LYNX

By Jalma Barrett
Photographs by Larry Allan

BLACKBIRCH PRESS, INC.
WOODBRIDGE, CONNECTICUT

Published by Blackbirch Press, Inc.
260 Amity Road
Woodbridge, CT 06525

e-mail: staff@blackbirch.com
Web site: www.blackbirch.com

Printed in the United States

10 9 8 7 6 5 4 3 2 1

Dedication
For Katlyn

–JB and LA

Library of Congress Cataloging-in-Publication Data
Barrett, Jalma.
Lynx / by Jalma Barrett : photographs by Larry Allan. — 1st ed.
    p.   cm. — (Wildcats of North America)
    Includes bibliographical references (p. 24) and index.
    Summary: Describes the lynx and its natural habitat, including physical traits, social life, survival instincts, birth and development, and interaction with humans.
    ISBN 1-56711-259-5 (lib. bdg. : alk. paper)
    1. Lynx—Juvenile literature. [1. Lynx.] I. Allan, Larry, ill. II. Title.
III. Series: Barrett, Jalma. Wildcats of North America.
QL737.C23B2658   1999
599.75'3—dc21   98-9881
                                                           CIP
                                                            AC

Contents

Introduction—Lynx: Cat in a Bow Tie

The lynx is sometimes called the Canadian lynx because it lives mostly in Canada. Lynx also live in Alaska and in forests in Washington, Oregon, Idaho, Montana, Colorado, Wyoming, and New England. A few lynx are still found in northern New York, Michigan, Wisconsin, and Minnesota. Lynx almost disappeared entirely in the eastern United States in the early twentieth century. They like to live in deep forests, especially evergreen woods that have rocky ledges, swamps, and thickets of brush. Lynx are also found in the forests of Eastern Europe and across Asia. They choose to live in hidden areas away from people. This is why less is known about their life-style and habits compared to other wildcats.

Where Lynx Are Most Common

CANADA

Rocky ledges and evergreen forests are two favorite lynx habitats.

The Lynx Body

The lynx is a close relative of the most common of all wildcats, the bobcat. Lynx are a little bigger than bobcats. Like bobcats, lynx have *tufts* (spikes of hair) on the ends of their ears. The lynx's tufts are longer than the bobcat's. They both have short tails, but lynx tails have black tips. Both lynx and bobcats have furry *ruffs* (collars of hair) around their faces called *muttonchops*. Lynx muttonchops are white with some bars of black. This makes the lynx look like it is wearing a bow tie! Both the lynx and bobcat have spots on their coats, but lynx spots are harder to see.

Lynx are light gray, with some brown to black hairs on their coats. They're especially known for the long black tufts on their ears and their big paws. Lynx weigh about 84 pounds (38 kilograms)— twice the size of a bobcat. Bobcats only weigh 38 pounds (17 kilograms). The average weight of a house cat is 10 to 12 pounds (4 to 6 kilograms). That makes a lynx seven or eight times the size of a pet cat!

Lynx are known for their large paws, short tails, and long black tufts on their ears.

A lynx's furry mutton-chops make it look like it's wearing a bow tie.
Inset: Lynx have short, bobbed tails with black on the tip.

A lynx's huge thickly furred paws spread as it walks in the snow.

Special Features

The most unique feature of the lynx is its huge paws. A lynx's paws are so big that it can run on top of snow without sinking. The hind (back) foot of a lynx can measure between 7 and 13 inches (17 to 33 centimeters) long. Their paw prints measure 3 to 4 inches (7 to 10 centimeters). In fresh powder snow, a lynx will only sink an inch or two. This gives them an advantage over other animals. A fox, for example, has feet that will sink into soft snow, slowing them down. The fox will sink into snow even though it weighs half as much as a lynx does. Big paws help the lynx to be a strong swimmer, too, just like flippers on a duck's feet help it swim better.

The claws of a lynx are much longer than a pet cat's. The lynx has four toes, like other cats. It walks with its claws pulled in—no claw marks show in its paw prints. Because of the heavy fur on its paws, lynx prints look really big, especially in heavy snow when the paw is spread open as much as possible. A lynx will sometimes leap as it follows along a trail, so there can be big gaps in its pattern of prints.

Like other types of cats, a lynx has excellent eyesight. Cat eyesight isn't affected by the dark the way a human's eyesight is. A cat's eyes have little mirror-like cells that magnify available light inside their eyes. This allows them to see clearly in very low light. The little cells are the reason people see a cat's eyes glow in the dark when bright light shines on them.

Lynx can't roar like lions and tigers. The bones in their voice boxes are connected so tightly they can't vibrate much. This means lynx produce smaller sounds. They tend to be silent, but they can scream or shriek. The screams end in a sort of crying sound, especially during mating season. They do purr when they are happy, just as a house cat does.

Lynx have excellent eyesight, especially in the dark.

Lynx mostly live alone.

Social Life

Lynx are shy and like to be alone. Being alone also helps lynx survive— it's easier for a single lynx to hunt food. A male will allow a female lynx with cubs to share his territory. Lynx carefully mark their territories to keep out competing lynx. They mark their territorial boundaries with urine sprayed on trees and stumps, and with *feces* (droppings). Sometimes they cover the feces with dirt and leaves. The scents they leave provide odor "information" about a lynx's territory. Other lynx recognize the smells and understand the territory boundaries. A lynx will keep the same territory for several years.

Lynx spend most of their day resting because they usually hunt and move at night. During the day they may hide among the roots of a tree that's fallen, on a low branch, or under a rocky ledge. They like to climb, but not too high. Sometimes they will leap down on passing prey.

A lynx is always on the lookout for possible prey.

Expert Hunters

Like most wildcats, lynx don't have a very good sense of smell. When they hunt, they rely on their ability to sneak up on prey. Their speed also helps them to chase their prey down. Lynx hunt both by *stalking* and by *ambushing* (hiding and attacking by surprise). They prey on rabbits, hares, small deer, and birds. A lynx's favorite food is the snowshoe hare. The hares often manage to escape a lynx's pounce. That is a quick, leaping attack. The pounce attack (jumping on and grabbing hold of their prey) is almost a lynx trade-mark. But the lynx is only successful in capturing its prey about once in every six attempts.

Hares make up about three-quarters of a lynx diet. Lynx survival is very closely connected to the snowshoe hare. The number of lynx living in an area depends a great deal on the population of these hares. Lynx may also eat the remains of caribou or moose they find. (Dead prey that has not been hunted by the animal that eats it is called *carrion*.) Lynx will also hide large prey they have not finished eating. This hidden meal is called a *cache*.

The lynx catches a snowshoe hare by jumping on, and grabbing hold of, it with large paws. This is called a pounce attack. Then the prey is killed by biting in the neck.

The Mating Game

Lynx will find mates in February or March. Several males might be attracted by a single female *in season* (ready to become pregnant). Usually, the males fight for the female. The most powerful male will win the right to mate. The female might mate with more than one male. Their litter of 1 to 6 cubs will be born in April or May, usually 63 to 70 days after mating.

Only a few weeks old, these cubs are alert and quite furry.

Cubs are raised only by their mothers.

Cubs

Cubs are born blind with spots and streaks on their fur. The den where they are born can be in a tree hollow, among rocks (like a small cave), or in scrub brush. Cubs will nurse for 4 to 5 months. They begin to go outside the den with their mother at about 2 months of age. Mothers do all the work of raising the young cubs. Males play no part at all in cub-raising. Cubs will stay with their mother until the following Spring—almost a full year. During this time they will play and be with other cubs. Part of their play teaches them about hunting. After a year, the cubs will have learned all the skills necessary to live on their own in the wild.

A lynx mother will teach her cubs all the skills they need to hunt and survive.

Learning by Playing

Young lynx learn the skills to live in the wild by playing in their surroundings and with other cubs.

Lynx habitats are being destroyed by human activity.

Lynx and Humans

Even though wolves and cougars are predators, humans are the lynx's main enemies. Sometimes lynx will attack farm livestock, but they are no real threat to people or their animals. The existence of lynx is threatened most by people who destroy their habitat. When people move near lynx territory, these shy creatures must find new homes. People also kill lynx for their long, silky fur. Lynx are protected by laws that prohibit hunting or trapping, but it's very difficult to enforce these laws.

The secluded forests that lynx call home are more and more being inhabited by people. As long as people protect these animals and give them their private space, the lynx will continue to thrive in North America and around the world.

Feline Facts

Name: Lynx

Scientific Name: *Felis lynx lynx*

Shoulder Height: 24" to 30" (60 to 76 cm)

Body Length: 28" to 36" (71 to 91 cm)

Tail Length: 2" to 6" (5 to 15 cm)

Weight: about 84 pounds (38 kilograms)

Color: Light gray

Reaches sexual maturity: Females at 21 months; males at 33 months

Females mate: Once every 2 years

Gestation (pregnancy period): 63 to 70 days

Litter Size: 1 to 6 cubs (usual size is 2 to 4)

Social Life: Lives alone

Favorite Food: Snowshoe hare
Hunts mainly at night

Habitat: Evergreen forests with rocky ledges, swamps, or brush thickets in Canada, very northern U.S. states, plus Colorado and Wyoming, Asia, and eastern Europe

Glossary

ambush To hide and then attack.

cache A hidden supply.

carrion Dead prey that was not hunted.

feces Bodily wastes; droppings.

habitat The place where an animal lives.

muttonchops Side whiskers.

pounce To jump on and suddenly grab hold of prey.

predator An animal that hunts other animals for food.

ruff A collar of hair.

stalking To hunt or track in a quiet, secret way; usually following prey.

tufts Spikes of hair.

Further Reading

Bonners, Susan. *Hunter in the Snow: The Lynx*. Boston: Little Brown & Co., 1994.

Hodge, Deborah. *Wild Cats: Cougars, Bobcats and Lynx*. Ontario: Kids Can Press, 1997.

London, Jonathan. *Let the Lynx Come In*. Cambridge, MA: Candlewick Press, 1996.

Schneider, Jost. *Lynx*. (Nature Watch). Minneapolis, MN: Carolrhoda Books, 1994.

Index